Geniune Relationship with God

Latasha Hobbs

TRILOGY CHRISTIAN PUBLISHERS
Tustin, CA

Trilogy Christian Publishers
A Wholly Owned Subsidiary of Trinity Broadcasting Network
2442 Michelle Drive
Tustin, CA 92780

Genuine Relationship with God

Copyright © 2024 by Latasha Hobbs

All Scripture quotations, unless otherwise noted, taken from THE HOLY BIBLE, NEW INTERNATIONAL VERSION®, NIV® Copyright © 1973, 1978, 1984, 2011 by Biblica, Inc.® Used by permission. All rights reserved worldwide.

Scripture quotations marked KJV are taken from the King James Version of the Bible. Public domain.

Scripture quotations marked NLT are taken from the Holy Bible, New Living Translation, copyright © 1996, 2004, 2015 by Tyndale House Foundation. Used by permission of Tyndale House Publishers, Inc., Carol Stream, Illinois 60188. All rights reserved.

All rights reserved, including the right to reproduce this book or portions thereof in any form whatsoever.

For information, address Trilogy Christian Publishing
Rights Department, 2442 Michelle Drive, Tustin, Ca 92780.

Trilogy Christian Publishing/ TBN and colophon are trademarks of Trinity Broadcasting Network.

For information about special discounts for bulk purchases, please contact Trilogy Christian Publishing.

Trilogy Disclaimer: The views and content expressed in this book are those of the author and may not necessarily reflect the views and doctrine of Trilogy Christian Publishing or the Trinity Broadcasting Network.

10 9 8 7 6 5 4 3 2 1

Library of Congress Cataloging-in-Publication Data is available.

ISBN 979-8-89333-477-7

ISBN 979-8-89333-478-4 (ebook)

I honor my Lord and Savior Jesus Christ, who is the head of my life!!!

I dedicate my book to

my mother Minnie Jean Hobbs,

who always told me to get some knee pads and pray,

and my cousin Apostle Joann McCauley,

who told me to sit and get quiet before God, and he will speak to you!

Giving Thanks

Especially to my sisters: Jassmin, you got me looking amazing, and Jamie, your creative design at your Crytique business made great keepsakes for the book. Thank you also to my other family members for being there, listening, and being my extra hands!!! A special thank you to my boys and granddaughter for always showing up and helping their mother and grandmother when needed. I am very grateful to God for you all!!!

My Pastor Embra and First Lady Stacie Patterson III

Mother Missionary Carol L. Bell

Kathy Marshall

Merilyn Banner

Sidney Zimmerman

Crytique Copy Shop

Contents

Introduction vii

Putting Together Your Altar (Special Spot)................... 1

Discipline 5

Reverance God-Worship.. 10

Release: Become Transparent 13

Count Up the Cost..20

Renew Your Mind..28

Putting It All Together 31

Why the Needed Items? 37

The Bible.. 39

The Journal... 42

The Timer 46

Conclusion 49

About the Author 59

Introduction

I am very thankful you purchased my book, *A Genuine Relationship with God*. This book is to help you develop a personal relationship with God. It does not matter where you are in your relationship with him; you can build from here, draw closer, and get to know him like you never did before. The plan is to start small and then grow your time. You have to discipline yourself to start to spend time with him, and then your desire will grow to spend more time. This is the purpose of my book: I will encourage you to work toward that, and then it will become your lifestyle.

When establishing any relationship, the foundation must be solid and intact so that, when life challenges arise, that relationship foundation is sturdy and allows you to go through any situation. How much more will it be when it comes to developing a genuine relationship with God? Think about builders that are about to construct a building. They will need to make sure the foundation is sturdy and the area is clean, removing debris and rocks that would hinder the foundation. In our spiritual walk, we have to do the same. We have to start at the basics by making sure our foundation is intact by asking God for forgiveness of our sins. By asking God for forgiveness for your sins, accepting God's son Jesus Christ as Lord and Savior of your life, and confessing with your mouth that Jesus Christ died on the cross for your sins and believing in your heart that he was raised from the dead in three days—you are saved from your sins and are in right standing with God! If you repent and confess with your mouth, then you are saved (Romans 10:9–11)!

As we build and develop our relationship with God, our discipline will turn to pleasure and then longing to be in God's presence.

As we know, all relationships start small, and the more time you spend with each other, the more it grows. It is no different with God, other than HE (God) been waiting for YOU (us) to draw closer to him. Draw nigh to God, and he will draw nigh to you (James 4:8).

Welcome to the family, and let's develop your relationship with our Heavenly Father, God!!!

Items Needed
  Bible
  Pen
  Notebook
  Chair/Table
  Quiet place
  Timer
  Pillows (knee pads)

Putting Together Your Altar (Special Spot)

Special Spot!

When you're looking for a place to meet God, you have to think about where you can sit and be quiet without being distracted. I will encourage you not to over-think the area but be mindful of where you can go and be relaxed but can be transparent with your Heavenly Father. The idea is to leave your needed items at your designated location. Why? Because when you show up to the area, it is always ready for you: you just have to get there! If it's your favorite Bible you take to church, get another one. The Bible you have in this designated area should be a study Bible along with a King James Version Bible. I have several versions of the Bible in my area, but I started with one study Bible. This place will become your special place over time.

For me, my spot is in my bedroom. I use a TV dinner table and a folding chair. I sit next to the window. I tend to keep the blind closed, but there was a time I had it open to be able to see the beauty of God's creation when I meditated on his Word.

Assignment

Go find your special spot!!!

Journal Pages

Where is your special spot? Will there be distractions? Can you leave your items?

LATASHA HOBBS

Discipline

What is Discipline?

Discipline means to "train oneself to do something in a controlled and habitual way" (New Oxford American Dictionary). Jesus told the disciples, "The spirit is willing but the flesh is weak" (Matthew 26:41). There are times when we will want to do a thing, but our flesh will not want to do it, and we have to discipline ourselves to do it until it becomes a habit to us. While we are doing this, sooner or later it will become desire. But it starts with discipline first!

You have to discipline yourself by getting up and being at the designated location at the time you set for yourself. For me, it was 5 a.m. It was a challenge at first, and I wanted something greater. I pushed and commanded my body (flesh) to do what it did not want to do, and I got up. Okay, let me be a little more honest: I had to force myself to get up. My husband at the time did not like noise when he was sleeping. At first I had an alarm by my bed that went off at 4:50 a.m. I turned it off ASAP and went right back to sleep. So, to make myself get out of bed, I set another alarm that was loud enough to wake us both up (he was mad by then, believe me), but I was up and out of bed, still tired, and I had my coffee already set to brew, so I walked past my special spot, which was always ready, to fetch my coffee. Finally, I was able to sit in my special spot. I forced myself to do what I desired to do, and it was not easy, but I put things in place to help force me to move to accomplish what I was desiring.

I will say it again, it will be a struggle. The flesh will not want to get up or discipline itself to change or stop doing anything to better itself, especially for the kingdom of God. You have to prepare for the challenges. How do you prepare for this situation? By having things in place such as a second alarm across the room or in another room and having your items in place and ready to overcome any obstacles or hindrances when it's time to spend time with God. You have to have a made-up mind and determination when you want something badly enough to put forth the effort to do something different.

In our discipline phase, we will just get up and show up! It might take some time to get that worked out. We acknowledge to God we are there and sit and be quiet before him.

This might sound silly, but I started with ten minutes. Yes, I did! It seems as if I was up and out before I knew it, but I was just as happy because I did it!

As time went on, I started to feel convicted. I had a sense I could sit for at least fifteen minutes, and before I knew it, I was spending twenty minutes, thirty minutes, and then a whole hour sitting and being quiet before the Lord. I will say that I wasn't hearing anything, but I had a peace within and noticed I started to have a desire to sit in my spot where I just knew God was going to meet me at my special spot. And now you will have a special spot too!!!

Side Note

If you already have a routine to pray and study but do not have a special spot, I encourage you to make one.

Journal Page

If you have a routine prayer schedule but not a designated location for it, find one. If you have both, reflect on how are you stopping and showing up every day. What's on your mind?

GENUINE RELATIONSHIP WITH GOD

Reverence God-Worship

One of my favorite Scriptures I am grateful for is Hebrews 4:16. The Bible says, "Let us then approach God's throne of grace with confidence, so that we may receive mercy and find grace to help us in our time of need." After Jesus died on the cross for our sins, we were able to go to God on our own without having a priest to speak or go before God on our behalf! Now we can make our requests known to God, but it's through his son, Jesus Christ: "Jesus answered, 'I am the way and the truth and the life. No one comes to the Father except through me'" (John 14:6). The Bible says the veil was ripped when our Lord Jesus Christ was hung on the cross for our sins, and since we accept him as our Savior, we then can go to the throne of grace boldly.

When we think of going boldly, we have to still reverence God correctly. He is our Heavenly Father!!! He tells us how to enter into his courts and presence. We did the first thing, which was to repent from our sins; we accepted his son Jesus Christ as our Lord and Savior into our life, and now we can go to our Heavenly Father, who is God, about our life, our family, and friends, about the things you see and hear about and talk to God about it from your point of view!!!

ALWAYS KNOW THAT GOD ALREADY KNOWS (1 John 3:20) BUT WANTS US TO TALK WITH HIM ABOUT OURSELVES.

When you're in your special spot and ready to talk (pray) to God, pour out to him. Do not hold back: you are there, he is there. It is the time to share and release our concerns to him. However, we must follow his instructions first. We don't run into his presence and start talking and not acknowledge him for who he is. Psalm 100:4 states, "Enter his gates with thanksgiving, and into his courts with praise: be thankful unto him, and bless his name." We are not formal like what you see or observe at church, but we have to start out thanking him and reverence who God is. When I show up, I do say these words that I have said many times: "Lord, here I am, again! I thank you for waking me up! You did not have to, but you did!" I thank him for life, health, and strength. I thank him that I wasn't woken up to any horrible news, and I thank him for keeping all hurt, harm, and danger away while I was sleeping because he is the God who withholds good and evil, and his eyes are going to and fro (2 Chronicles 16:9). I make it known to God what Acts 17:28 tells us: "In him we live and move and have our being"!!! I start out thanking God! Lastly, on reverencing God, check out Matthew 6:9–13. The disciples wanted to know how to pray, and Jesus gave them a model prayer. This is the Lord's Prayer. Many people were taught this prayer when they were children, and they say this prayer over and over, but it becomes a ritual prayer and they are just saying words. The Lord's Prayer is instead meant to be a format for how to *arrange* our prayers.

The Lord's Prayer model tells us to start and reverence God, then we move to ask for forgiveness for anything and everything that we might have done and things we do not know were done. (God is omniscient, which means God is all-knowing: we will never get by or hide anything from him, so we have to always come clean and be transparent. When you think about establishing a genuine relationship with God, come clean and keep the pathway clear to him.) He wants us to have a solid relationship with him, and he made that possible with himself through his son Jesus Christ.

Again, when we approach God, we have to reverence him and praise him for who he is in our life. It has to be done to get his attention because you're disciplining yourself to be in his presence daily, and you're taking the time to get to know him. He told us what he likes and wants and what he wants us to do, and we have to accept his instructions when we go to the throne of grace boldly the way he wants us to. God said in Psalm 22:3 (KJV) that he inhabits the praises of his people.

Release: Become Transparent

Release

It's time to get ready to release to God!!! We have a clear pathway by repenting and accepting his son Jesus Christ as Lord and Savior, and then we can enter his presence with thanksgiving, and now we can release our cares to God (1 Peter 5:7–10)!!!

I shared that in the beginning we have to discipline ourselves to get up and have set the time to pray to our Heavenly Father.

Now when we release our prayers to God, it's still in the same lane; we are in a conversation with God. We are sharing our concerns from our point of view with an all-knowing God! If you're going to have a meaningful and effective conversation or prayer life, you have to speak and then get quiet before God and give God time to speak back to you. Once again, it's a discipline, and you have to be consistent and know what you're doing is not in vain! Hebrews 11:6 (NLT) says, "Anyone who wants to come to him must believe that God exists and that he rewards those who sincerely seek him." The point I'm trying to stress is to be consistent in your devotional time with God.

When you talk to God, pour out to him about everything in your heart. Tell God about everything: the good, the bad, and the ugly. Now, there was a time I was not on my knees when I was talking to God! I was sitting in my chair at the table. I might have coffee at times, but I was talking to him and sharing my frustration, disappointment, happiness, and sadness. The key thing to take away was that I was talking to him as if he were sitting right in front of me. There were many times the devil made me feel I was crazy doing this, but I kept showing up, seeking God, and going to my special spot. Isaiah 65:24 (NLT) says, "I will answer them before they even call to me. While they are still talking about their needs, I will go ahead and answer their prayers!"

And again, remember Hebrews 11:6: he is a rewarder!

While you're there talking to God, don't just be rambling because you're on a time limit. We want our conversation with God to be the effectual fervent prayer of a righteous person (James 5:16). If something is truly pressing on your heart, your conversation with God is meaningful.

As you know, conversation is twofold. There is a sender and a receiver. When you speak as the sender, then you stop and allow God to speak back, and you become the receiver. That's why we set a timer. The plan is to allow the same amount of time for God to speak back to you. Be willing to open up and listen to what God has to say.

Just know when God speaks back, we are listening for a still small voice. That is the reason the time of your devotional is crucial to help limit noise and distraction. When it is God's time to talk to you, you have to understand that just being quiet before him and waiting and anticipating our Heavenly Father to speak back is very critical and needed. In 1 Kings 19:11–12, Elijah was waiting to hear from God. This Scripture says,

> And he said, Go forth, and stand upon the mount before the Lord. And, behold, the Lord passed by, and a great and strong wind rent the mountains, and brake in pieces the rocks before the Lord; but the Lord was not in the wind: and after the wind an earthquake; but the Lord was not in the earthquake: and after the earthquake a fire; but the Lord was not in the fire: and after the fire a still small voice. (KJV)

And it was so when Elijah heard it. The voice can come in many forms, but for the most part, it will be in a still small voice, and it will be lined with his words. The time we spend with him will help us have an ear to hear him speak to us.

You will journal everything that comes to your heart and mind, even about how you felt during your silence. I will talk more later about the journal.

Yes, I am repeating this: you will feel crazy and foolish. I did! It is a trick of the enemy to make you stop and not put practical things in place to grow in God. All thoughts will come to your mind, but I encourage you to do this, and you will see God show up and talk to you, and you will soon build a relationship with your Heavenly Father in a way you never knew him before, and you will learn who you are from his point of view, all starting in your special spot. So yet again, block the thoughts out: all you have is fifteen to twenty minutes to talk, and when the timer goes off, you're done! The rest of the time is for God to talk. However long you talked, he gets the same amount of time. You sit there and be quiet, blocking everything out of your mind. Close your eyes and listen. Write down in your journal what comes to your heart and mind. Suppose a song comes to mind. Write it down, and after the timer goes off, go and listen to the song, write the words down, and meditate on what the song was saying to you! The notebook is there to reflect what happened in that time you spent with God, and you can reflect throughout your journey. (Especially when distraction comes into your life, if you have it written down in your journal, you will thank me later.)

Just think for a moment if you ever planted a seed and placed the cup or container in the window to grow. I am sure you kept going back to look at the seed for something to happen, and every day you went, there was nothing. I am sure you kept watering the plant and allowing the sun to shine on it. If you were anything like me, you became frustrated. As time went on, you finally noticed a small green piece of something coming out of the dirt. It was finally growing. When you continue to show up and put into practice what is mapped out in God's Word and apply it to your life, you too will see the manifestation of God's hand working within your life. It is the same way by taking God's words, spending time with him, and applying his Word to our life. We will soon see the growth in us if we are doers of God's word (James 1:22)!

My Story

I was in my spot talking to God about a situation I was dealing with, and I was asking our Heavenly Father to help me not to go back into the situation again. I remember telling God not to let me go, to keep me close to him so I would not get entangled in that situation again. I wanted to be free, and if he got me out of that situation, I would praise him and testify about it. I shared with God I enjoyed what I was doing, but I knew it was wrong and I needed help. I told God I wanted to be free from my sin. I did not hide my true feelings about the situation because God knew how I felt about it. After I acknowledged God and was transparent to HIM how I was feeling about my situation, I told him in my secret quiet time that I needed him to help me to bring me out and then I needed him to keep me. Then the timer went off. I had to stop talking, but I wanted to pour out more, and I remember I was crying and everything. But STOP! As I was getting myself together and cleaning my face (I had towels and Kleenex nearby), I got quiet. I remember this as if it were yesterday: a song was starting to ring in my heart. I was trying to block it out because I was trying to focus on a word from the Lord!!! Then the song came back to me, and I felt God's presence on me as if his arms were wrapped around me, rocking me. As I was listening to words and I felt his presence, I started to cry more because our Heavenly Father was telling me through the song, "I will never let go of your hand!!!" God heard what I was saying to him, and he spoke back to me. It was not the first time I sat down or the second time, but as I was consistent in his presence, he came and spoke back to me.

With me showing up regularly, I was showing God I wanted him and not just what he could do for me. I want to be a child of God. I want to know who my Heavenly

Father is, for he told us we were created in his image (Genesis 1:27). He also told us in Jeremiah 1:5, "Before I formed you in the womb I knew you" and in Jeremiah 29:11, "'For I know the plans I have for you,' declares the Lord, 'plans to prosper you and not to harm you, plans to give you hope and a future.'" I want to experience these plans as a child of God and see who is this person, and having a relationship with our Heavenly Father will bring that transformation in my/your life. (Getting to know who you are like you never did before!)

Yes, I am saying it again: the morning is less distracting. "In the morning, Lord, you hear my voice; in the morning I lay my requests before you and wait expectantly" (Psalm 5:3).

Count Up the Cost

Count Up the Cost: Is It Worth It?

The Bible tells us to count up the cost (Luke 14:28)! For the most part, people tend to weigh out the pros and cons, ponder over whether it is worth it or not, and don't even bother with temporal decisions. People will put years of dedication to what they want to accomplish here on earth, and this life is considered a vapor (James 4:14). We should build our lives on things eternal (Matthew 6:19–21). Let me help with weighing this out: "What you do for God will last, period!!!" (2 Corinthians 4:18). Having a solid relationship with God will strengthen your spiritual walk and relationship with God, and then you can go help someone else. Jesus told Peter to get himself together and then go help his brother and sisters (Luke 22:32). We are ambassadors of Christ (2 Corinthians 5:20). While we are here on this earth, we are working for God to reach people. If we have a genuine relationship with God, we will be like his son Jesus Christ and be about his Father's business (Luke 2:48–49). We are to be holy (1 Peter 1:15–16), we are to be loving, we are to have the same mindset as God's son, Jesus Christ (Philippians 2:5).

Look at your life, your loved ones, your friends, the world! When you have a solid foundation rooted and grounded with God through his son Jesus Christ, you can go boldly to the throne of grace and speak to God on your own behalf (Hebrew 4:16).

I can pray with you and for you, but just know when you develop a relationship with God and you start praying to our Heavenly Father about your situation, you will be able to tell your story a lot better than I can. Yes, count up the cost in this journey as something you're willing to discipline yourself for!

My Story

I was in a dead state in my life, but I was going to church and was involved in many activities. If the church doors were open, I was there. I got to the point where I was given keys to the church, I was holding positions in the church, and I even held titles. I was faithful to the business and work of the church and showed up for people, but my life was not lining up with what I was teaching. On one hand, I was a little naïve to the point of thinking I was building a relationship with God because I was working in the church, and on the other hand, I knew I was wrong in some areas of my life, but I didn't heed the warnings that were coming forth and disregarded the messages, saying they were not for me. As time went on, I stayed in that state, still working and doing and serving in the name of the Lord. Until the cover was pulled back by God!!!

At the beginning of my warnings, the Lord was bringing a story to my memory all the time, which was about Mary and Martha. Martha was busy preparing the dinner for Jesus because he was coming to visit. When Jesus was drawing closer, Martha was feeling the pressure of not being prepared and ready for the event. As for Mary, she was preparing for him to come as well, but not the same way.

God was trying to get my attention by bringing the story of Mary and Martha back to my remembrance, but I was too busy and was not grasping what he was trying to get me to focus on, and all my energy was in the wrong area. When Jesus finally made it to Martha and Mary's home, Martha said to Jesus, "Tell Mary to help me prepare for the dinner!" In Jesus's loving way, he told Martha, "I am not going to stop her from doing what is best." She chose to do the better of the two things, which was being at Jesus's feet (Luke 10:38–42). That was not the case for me: I chose to stay busy, and I got too involved in doing the work, and over time I got worse. I became busy and never applied the Word to my life. Even though I was around the church and members all the time, I was like Martha, and then I became like the Pharisees. I looked good on the outside but was dead on the inside (Matthew 23:27).

If I had paid attention to God's warnings presented to me, I could have corrected my sin by repenting to him and would have not drifted so far away from him and gotten comfortable in my sin. Since I did not, I continued in my sin. I was comfortable with it. I felt bad, but I did not stop. I was still involved in church activities, but I never stopped. One day God pulled back the covers of my life and showed everyone that my spirit was not lining up for the work and positions I was upholding in the church. God exposed how entangled I was in a situation, and he was not pleased with my lifestyle. I was grounded from positions, titles, and the work in the church. I had to step down from it all. I was not asked to leave the church; I was to sit. I was asked to resign, and I did. I started to hit and miss church a lot. And God came and asked me a question:

"What are you going to do?"

I started to reflect on my life. I gave my life to God when I was nineteen years old and was on fire for him. I walked away from the world because I had enough of the life that I experienced early on and wanted no more of what the world was offering. I could not go back. Everyone in my world knew I was confessing I was a saint, and if I walked away, I would have been a fish out of water. I did not know how I got here, other than I got complacent with my lifestyle, lost my focus, and became stagnant in my spiritual walk. I went to church and I attended the classes. I heard what they were saying and I enjoyed the music. So where did I go wrong? How did I get stuck? I put none of what I heard into practice anymore and was not truly connected to the Father (John 15:1–8).

The devil did not care I was working in the church and attending church. He did not care about me having my name on the church member list, he did not care I listened to the Word of God or played Christian music—he does not care about that!!! He had me blinded to what matters. What matters is putting my focus back on God, lining my life up with his Word, and doing what Jesus told Martha was the better between the two choices: being at Jesus's feet and applying his Word to my life. He wants me to present my body as a living sacrifice holy and acceptable to God (Romans 12:1–2). God's Word says we are in the world but not of the world (John 17:11, 14–15). He also says, "Therefore, if anyone is in Christ, the new creation has come: The old has gone, the new is here!" (2 Corinthians 5:17). Finally, he also says, "Be ye doers of the word, and not hearers only" (James 1:22, KJV).

I separated from God due to my sinful state. I was spiritually dead, and I knew it deep down within myself, but God's love made me face myself, and then he asked me the question: "What are you going to do?" I had to decide what I was going to do. I had not counted up the cost. I have been saved for years, and all I knew at this point was the church life, and I had to decide whom I was going to serve: God or the devil!

I answered God's question: I wanted to be right, and I wanted to be saved. I counted up the cost, and I decided to do what I had to do to get myself back on track and stay on track with the Lord!

I ask the same question to you.

"What are you going to do?"

Journal Page

What are you going to do? Reflect on what you need to let go of or clean up in your life. Revisit broken vows. What are your thoughts?

GENUINE RELATIONSHIP WITH GOD

Renew Your Mind

I'M ALL IN!!

"I'm all in" was my answer to God. I was going to do this salvation lifestyle the way God has mapped out and from this point on. I was determined to know God in a way I never knew him before. God wants you and me to accept Jesus Christ as our Lord and Savior. He wants us to have an abundant life here on earth (John 10:10). Psalm 34:8 says, "Taste and see that the Lord is good." I decided I was going to do what God said and do it to the best of my ability.

2 Corinthians 5:17 (KJV) states, "Therefore if any man be in Christ, he is a new creature: old things are passed away; behold, all things are become new." I am here to share with you some of the same steps that will help you to develop a genuine relationship with God! You will see a true transformation in your life and your heart. You will walk differently and talk differently, and your desires will line up with God's will for you!

The Scripture that came to mind was about renewing your mind: "Let this mind be in you, which was also in Christ Jesus" (Philippians 2:5, KJV). I had to repent

GENUINE RELATIONSHIP WITH GOD

and do my first works, again. This cleared my pathway to God, and I knew the things I needed to do and put into place to get back on track. What I had to do was establish a relationship with God and turn from the ways that I knew were wrong. I became desperate and started to act like Jacob: I was going to get in his presence and not let him go until he blessed my soul (Genesis 32:22–30)!! I started to practice all the teachings I heard about and kept my eyes on the Lord, not for a position or to receive titles in the church, but to be acceptable to God. I wanted to be all I was created to be. The only title I was striving to hold and making sure I held was the title of a saint, a believer, a Christian. I wanted to be upright in the sight of our Heavenly Father, and I was going to live up to the name!!! I answered God's question of "What are you going to do?" with "I am going to walk the walk, talk the talk, and be who God said I am: Be ye holy for I am holy (1 Peter 1:15–16)!!!" Heaven and Hell are real, and eternity is forever, and I did not want my soul to go to hell because I would not put the time in to be a true saint. I put countless time in over the years to receive certifications and associate degrees, which led to my bachelor's degrees and working on a Master's. That will not matter at the end of time. My degree might be beneficial here on earth, but what I do for Christ will last, and how much more will I need to put toward my soul that will live forever? The Bible says all things will pass away in Matthew 24:34–35 (KJV): "Verily I say unto you, This generation shall not pass, till all these things be fulfilled. Heaven and earth shall pass away, but my words shall not pass away." We must make sure that whatever we are doing while we are here on earth, we are building, connecting, and lining ourselves up with God to have a genuine relationship with him.

When you renew your mind, you have to be like Joshua when he was talking to the children of Israel: "Choose you this day whom ye will serve" (Joshua 24:15, KJV). I chose God, and I will do whatever I need to do to make that happen. From that day till now, I guard myself and I will not get too busy like Martha. I resist the devil so he can flee from me, I study to show my self-approval, I establish a special spot in my home where I still meet God, and now I am doing what Jesus told Peter, going back and helping my brothers and sister to do the same (Luke 22:32).

Putting It All Together

It is Time to Put It All Together!!!

You have decided to create a routine for yourself to make time available to develop a time to be in God's presence for you and him to conversate about you, your concerns, and others—all with the expectation that God will conversate back to you about you and that you will learn of him. He will show you himself while he opens your eyes to you!!! He will show you how much he loves you through his son Jesus Christ, and Jesus Christ will show you how much he loves you by sending the Holy Ghost to live in your heart and guide you and teach you and make the word of God alive in your life, which will be a mirror to you and allow you to see yourself from his eyes and draw you closer to him!

I know that was a mouthful. Let me say it again. God will show you how much he loves you (John 3:16), which was shown when he sent his son to earth to die on the cross for your sins, and when his son Jesus Christ ascended to heaven, he sent the Holy Ghost to live inside of us to teach, guide (John 14:16), and bring God's Word to life in our hearts (Hebrews 4:12).

In this phase of putting things together, I would like to speak about The Lord's Prayer once again, which is a prayer model and format for people. God is your Heavenly Father and my Heavenly Father, along with all the other believing saints across this world. The Lord's Prayer starts by acknowledging God as our Father! He has a lot of children, and we have to interact with his other children, who are our brothers and sisters in Christ. As we all interact with each other, we are to help and draw strength from one another. You ask, "Where are you going with this, Latasha?" The Bible says, "Not forsaking the assembling of ourselves together, as the manner of some is; but exhorting one another: and so much the more, as ye see the day approaching" (Hebrews 10:25, KJV). I am saying if you're not part of a Bible-believing church, you need to be! As the Scripture states in Hebrews 10:25, we are required to exhort one another!

First Corinthians 12:12–27 (KJV) states, "For as the body is one, and hath many members, and all the members of that one body, being many, are one body: so also is Christ. For by one Spirit are we all baptized into one body, whether we be Jews or Gentiles, whether we be bond or free; and have been all made to drink into one Spirit." You are needed in the body of Christ, and you

GENUINE RELATIONSHIP WITH GOD

need to be connected to God's family for your strength. You cannot be a hidden child of God!!! What you do in secret in your special spot is your intimate time with your Heavenly Father, and he will reward you (Hebrews 11:6). He also says in Matthew 6:6 (KJV), "But thou, when thou prayest, enter into thy closet, and when thou hast shut thy door, pray to thy Father which is in secret; and thy Father which seeth in secret shall reward thee openly." But you are not a secret Christian; you are not on an island by yourself. With that being said, again, you need to be part of a church under a pastor who is after God's heart and will teach and instruct and oversee your soul. When you get around your spiritual siblings, God shows up even more. He says, "For where two or three gather in my name, there am I with them" (Matthew 18:20).

The "putting it all together" phase is instructing you to seek God by finding a church home if you do not have one. Not a church home where your friends or family are attending, but a church home where God wants you to go. Now, I will say if you're not going anywhere, go ahead and start visiting a church with your family or friend, but seek God to lead you to where he wants you to be. "In all thy ways acknowledge him, and he shall direct thy paths" (Proverbs 3:6, KJV).

To have a genuine relationship with anyone, you need to be able to experience them in different settings, and you will learn that God does not change. You will learn that when you are around your spiritual siblings, you draw strength from and give strength to each other. As time goes on, you will be spending time with God in your special spot, and you'll be attending church and fellowshipping with your spiritual siblings with God in the midst of it all. God will allow you to start to see yourself as you never would have known YOURSELF, and you will know God like never before in different settings.

Assignment

When you attend church, take your Bible (not the Bible from your special spot), paper, and pen. Take notes, writing down the Scriptures and whatever the speaker says that pulls at your heart: the good, the bad, and the ugly. If it made you mad, write it all down. If it made you glad, write it down. Then you will go to your special spot and reflect and revisit the message and talk with God about it. Why does it make you mad? Why does it make you glad? Then you write your responses in your journal.

Next Sunday or next time you're at church, do the same thing.

The Bible tells us to meditate on God's Word, and it tells us to study to show our approval, and it tells us to pray. As we put all this together, we will be who God calls us to be (Romans 8:29).

GENUINE RELATIONSHIP WITH GOD

Journal Page

Do you take notes at church? Do you take a Bible? Do you use a phone? Why?

Why the Needed Items?

I have given suggested items to have at your special spot for you to have when you show up. It is great to have these items always there when you get there. Throughout the book I spoke on each item, but I want to explain the importance of having each item. When you create your spot, I encourage you not to have anything that could cause distraction and draw your attention away from the reason you are there. With that being said, NO TECHNOLOGY!!!

Technology is linked to everything we are connected to. Our emails, Facebook, Instagram, video games, text messages, you name it, are connected to the world through our technology. When you arrive at our special spot, you shut off the world for some time to get the most out of the allotted time you set for yourself.

Once again, the suggested items to have at your spot are below:

- The Holy Bible—two versions (I recommend KJV and Life Application Study Bible NLT)

- Notebook for personalized journaling
- A timer
- Pillows
- Pen
- Kleenex
- Table

The Bible

The Bible: Holy or Nothing

The Bible is God-breathed (2 Timothy 3:16); all the authors who wrote the Bible were led by the Holy Spirit. The words of the Lord are pure words, like silver refined in a furnace on the ground, or like gold purified seven times (Psalm 12:6), and 2 Peter 1:21 states, "For prophecy never had its origin in the human will, but prophets, though human, spoke from God as they were carried along by the Holy Spirit."

For me, the Bible is God's instructions on his standards and expectations. The Bible teaches us who God is and how much he loves us. We learn what he likes and dislikes.

I have a Bible in my special spot to read and study. I open the Bible to read what God already said about a situation I might be going through. This tends to start a conversation with God about my situation. The conversation never changes what he said already, but I work out and adjust to what he says by sharing my thoughts and concerns.

I already shared that when God was trying to tell me I was too busy in the church and he kept bringing the story of Mary and Martha to me, I read the story. I did not seek God to see what he was saying to me about the story. When we read God's words, we have to pray and ask him to allow the Word to come alive to us. We are to meditate on his Word (Joshua 1:8), and his Word will speak to us. We cannot read the Bible like any other book. First Corinthians 2:14 says, "The person without the Spirit does not accept the things that come from the Spirit of God but considers them foolishness, and cannot understand them because they are discerned only through the Spirit." We have to be connected to God and seek God to bring the truth to us about his words. When we are in our special spot and we read God's Word, we have to pray and ask God to help us to comprehend his Word, and then we have to meditate on his words. We are not there to read to say, "I read the Bible." We are there to experience communion and learn of God, and he will show you YOURSELF, and he will show you HIMSELF through his WRITTEN WORD.

I have a study Bible in my special spot that I leave there, and I have a King James Version as well. There are many translations of the Bible. Many of the newer translations take out a lot of God's words to make you understand it better, but it takes away what God was saying. That is why I keep a King James Version there.

I have my Bible I take back and forth to church with me on Sundays, when I do not go to my special spot. Once again, when I do show up to my special spot later, everything is always there.

Another thing I would encourage you to do is when you're at church, take your Bible and have a notebook and pen with you. When the message is going forth, write the Scripture down and the topic for the message. Write anything and everything down that pulls at your heart. Don't write too much that distracts you from the message, but take notes. On Monday go to your special spot, open up your Sunday notes, and revisit that message. Read the Scriptures, and whatever jumps out at you, talk to the Lord about it. Seek the Scripture and see if the Lord already said something about it. Because if something jumped out at you, the Lord wants to talk to you about that situation. Revelation 3:20 states, "Here I am! I stand at the door and knock. If anyone hears my voice and opens the door, I will come in and eat with that person, and they with me." When points of the message jump out at you when God's Word is going forth, take heed of it because God is trying to work in that area in your life, and you don't want to ignore that. That is why you need to write it down: the devil will not help remind you what you heard, and your flesh will not want to discipline itself to study and seek God for nothing. That is why it is important for you to take notes at church.

Assignment

If you have not gotten a good study Bible, get one and pray and ask God for the right translation. I like the Life Application Study Bible NLT, and I also use the King James Version Bible. I also like the Message Bible and The Amplified Bible.

The Journal

Your Journal

The notebook is to journal everything that comes to your heart and your mind. I encourage you to date all your journal entries. Your journal is for you to write in and then go back and reflect on your growth during this process. I wrote out what I wanted to talk to God about in my journal to keep me focused. (You're on a time limit.) I wrote all the names of my loved ones, my friends, and cares of the world on the back of my notebook. I was able to pray for them daily because I have them right there listed. As stated earlier, I journaled how God was silent. In conversation with people, there are times we just listen and don't give a word, and that is just as important as saying something. It is just knowing God is there and he is listening to me. I wrote, "God listened and he was there."

Journal Page

How hard is it for you to sit and be quiet before God? Have you listed the names of your loved ones on the back of your journal?

GENUINE RELATIONSHIP WITH GOD

The Timer

The timer is just what it is: a timer. It is to keep time and keep you on track with your time with God. The timer is used to cut you off from talking to God, mainly. We don't want to be babbling and retelling our story or our problem over and over to God, pleading our case. He knows already, and he wants us to cast our burdens on him. He wants us to still be away in our secret spot and pray without ceasing, but we have to share our concerns and then allow him time to speak back to us (and accept he might be silent too). We have to train ourselves to do that, and the timer will help us to say what we need to say and let it go when the timer goes off and then allow God adequate time (set the timer to the same amount of time) to speak back to us.

As it was stated earlier, you set the time for yourself, and when the timer goes off, you're done. Reset the timer for the Lord to talk, and you sit there quietly before him. I shared that my time started short, and as time went on, I told myself I could do at least fifteen minutes, but then the time got longer and longer. I started to see changes in myself, and the peace that I had was unexplainable.

My Story

I have been going to my special spot for some time now, and it was a struggle at times, but I was consistent. When I had my little routine down, I noticed I was going back there outside of my set time (5 a.m.). I would get my daily activities done, and instead of sitting down to watch television, I went to my special spot and talked to the Lord about my day. I still had a timer, especially if I was praying, because praying is talking to God. If I talked, I had to stop and allow him to talk back. I noticed I was longing to get to my special spot and meet God. I felt I was in seventh heaven. My whole demeanor changed. My connection with my brothers and sisters in Christ was different. I loved who I was. I loved God's people, and I was handling situations differently. God has changed me from the inside out and has shown me who I can be if I stay connected to him.

In fact, when I was talking to God about myself and my family, one day the Lord told me to stop coming as much to my special spot because I was neglecting being present with my husband and my children. I was like, "What? What do you mean, God?"

I shared my story with you about how it was hard to get started going to my special spot. But when I started, over time God did come and meet me there. I had to work it out. The timer kept me on track. But God did make me stop spending my family time in my special spot, even though I was longing to be there to talk to him about my day. God loved me so much that he knew I had a family that I had to go tend to and be present with them too—even though I felt because I did all my motherly and wifely duties at home, I was free to steal away and be with the Lord. I enjoyed my special spot so much and my interaction with God, but God had to remind me I was a mother, and my boys needed me and my husband wanted to interact with his wife.

Conclusion

A genuine relationship with God is designed to give practical ways to build a meaningful relationship with God. I shared my story to show why I even started this journey, and since I have been doing this constantly, my life has changed. I have not reached the life of perfection because I am in the land of the living, but I am striving and still working on myself. I do know one thing: I see God as a loving father who loves me enough to deal with me and allow me to see myself through his eyes, all while I keep my eyes focused on him through his son, Jesus Christ.

I have given some suggestions throughout the book to guide you and Scriptures to help encourage you to be determined to draw closer to God through his son Jesus Christ, knowing he is there waiting for you. If you can follow it like I did, it is great. It's working for me, and I'm still practicing this same regiment today. The more you draw nigh to God, the more he will draw nigh to you. God said in Hebrews 11:6 (KJV), "He [God] is a rewarder of them that diligently seek him," and if you have the hunger and thirst to know God, do the suggested guide or create a plan and then be consistent in your pursuit; you will obtain a sense of peace and love on the inside that the world did not give or take away. I again ask you what you are going to do and to count up the cost. Build your life on eternal things, not things on this earth that will pass away because they are temporal.

Reminisce for a moment.

If you have been in a relationship with someone and wanted to get to know them, what did you do? I am sure you did what I did, which was to make time to spend time with that person. I remember holding the phone when neither of us was even saying anything, and when we said, "I'm about to hang up," neither of us hung the phone up until the other one did it first. But neither of us wanted to do it. So, one of us finally said, "No, you do it," and the other said, "No, you do it." Then we counted 1–2–3, and then we both hung up the phone. The point I am making is we strived to put the time into getting to know each other and did what it took, even if it was silly. I held on to the phone even when I did not hear anything from the other person, but I knew they were there. It's okay when we don't hear God say anything to us, but I believed he was there, and it's just good to know he is there. We made the time to be with that person because we wanted to know them better with the hope of becoming closer. How much more would that be for our Heavenly Father, who showed us he loved us so much by making it possible for us to come boldly to his throne and plead our case to him from our point of view?

We put countless hours into earthly success such as education, work, business, and earthly relationships. How much more should we build a relationship with our Heavenly Father? I will never say that because you have a relationship with God, your life will be perfect. It WILL NOT because you are a child of God. (But in him you will have a peace that no one can explain, and you will be considered a peculiar person [1 Peter 2:9]!!!) You will notice when you study the Word of God that all God's people had some kind of heartache going on in their lives for some sort due to their own doing or not, but God was with them. God fought for them. That will be your story of having a genuine relationship with God. (Yes, I know God reigns on the just as well as the unjust, but it is different being one of his children.) One thing you should know or be reminded of is the devil will magnify any and every situation you're dealing with. He will try his best to get your focus off God and distract you like he did Peter when he was walking on the water toward Jesus Christ (Matthew 14:30–33). The time you spend with God builds your relationship with him and strengthens your faith in him. Just know nothing changed in your life other than you put God first and made time, and life was just magnified by the devil to get you to lose focus, and guess what? YOU DID NOT or WILL NOT BECAUSE OF YOUR RELATIONSHIP WITH GOD!!!

It all started to happen because you built on a solid foundation of his son Jesus Christ, who will never leave you or forsake you. (Hebrews 13:5). God will fight for you. Yes, weapons will form against you, but they will not prosper (Isaiah 54:17). As the young generation at times says, "Life be lifing," but we can rest assured we can go to our Heavenly Father in prayer and tell him all about it boldly! God loves us more than we will ever know and shows that when he sends his son (John 3:16), he will show us individually when we start seeking him one-on-one. I pray my book *A Genuine Relationship with God* helps you make your relationship with God your own, and I hope my stories will show no one has made it to heaven yet if they are on this earth.

I love you with the love of God!

Latasha

GENUINE RELATIONSHIP WITH GOD

Where Do You Go from Here?

LATASHA HOBBS

Names of Family Members

LATASHA HOBBS

Concerns of the World

LATASHA HOBBS

About the Author

Latasha Hobbs is a devoted follower of Jesus Christ. She accepted Jesus Christ as her Lord and Savior at the age of nineteen. She rededicated her life in 2016 when she believed the Lord showed her himself and she experienced him in a way she never had before. Latasha attends House of Faith COGIC in Decatur, IL, under the leadership of her Pastor Embra Patterson III and First Lady Stacie Patterson. Latasha has served in many areas of the church, serving both the Lord and his people. She was called into ministry in 2005 as a licensed evangelist missionary and assisted the ministry. Her transformation in 2016 lit a fire in her to teach and minister the word of God to all humankind to help them see God loves them and makes provision for them to be in a personal relationship with him, understanding a true relationship with God is more than church attendance.

Latasha is a mother of four boys and grandmother of two granddaughters. She has been very involved in her children's lives from their education to their sports, as well as the development of their relationship with God. She is an RN with a BSN. She works in public schools as a nurse and a mental health nurse.

Printed in the USA
CPSIA information can be obtained
at www.ICGtesting.com
CBHW071955090724
11357CB00006B/131